THE WATER CYCLE

For Kids

Copyright © 2022 Samuel John

Planet Earth is made up of three-quarters of water.

Water is always in constant motion. This is what we call the **water cycle**.

WATER CYCLE

>> The process of water circulation between different parts of the **hydrosphere**.

Water is found in nature in three different states: liquid, solid and gas.

SOLID
Ice or snow

LIQUID
Seas, rivers, lakes and oceans

GAS
Cloud formation

- Water is irreplaceable.

- There would be no life without water. Plants, animals and us humans would cease to exist.

- For that reason, it should not be wasted. Also, we must take care of the lakes, the rivers, the seas and the oceans.

EVAPORATION

The Sun heats the sea, lakes, and rivers.

The water evaporates and goes from a liquid to a gaseous state due to this heating.

It turns into water vapor and moves up to the atmosphere.

CONDENSATION

The water transformed into vapor moves up to the atmosphere, cools off, and concentrates into tiny water drops that form clouds.

This condensation process causes the water to change back from a gaseous state to a liquid one.

The water condensed and converted into a cloud continues to move to another place, carried by the wind.

PRECIPITATION

We already know that clouds are made up of tiny drops of water suspended in the air.

When there is a large accumulation of water, the drops become too large and heavy and end up falling and returning to the ground.

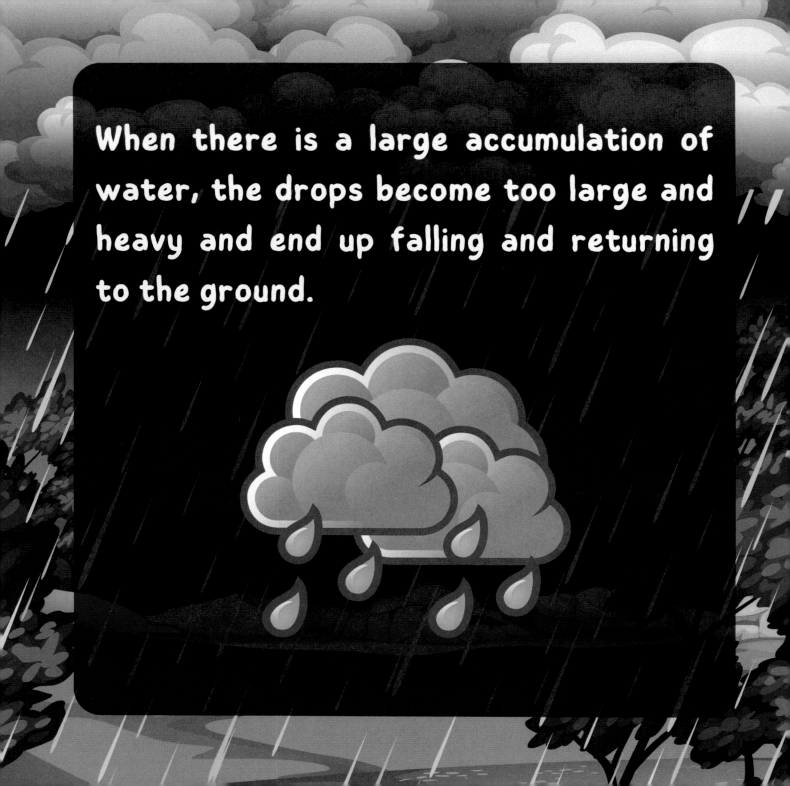

Precipitation of water normally occurs in a liquid state, but due to certain weather conditions, it can be in solid form: snow and hail.

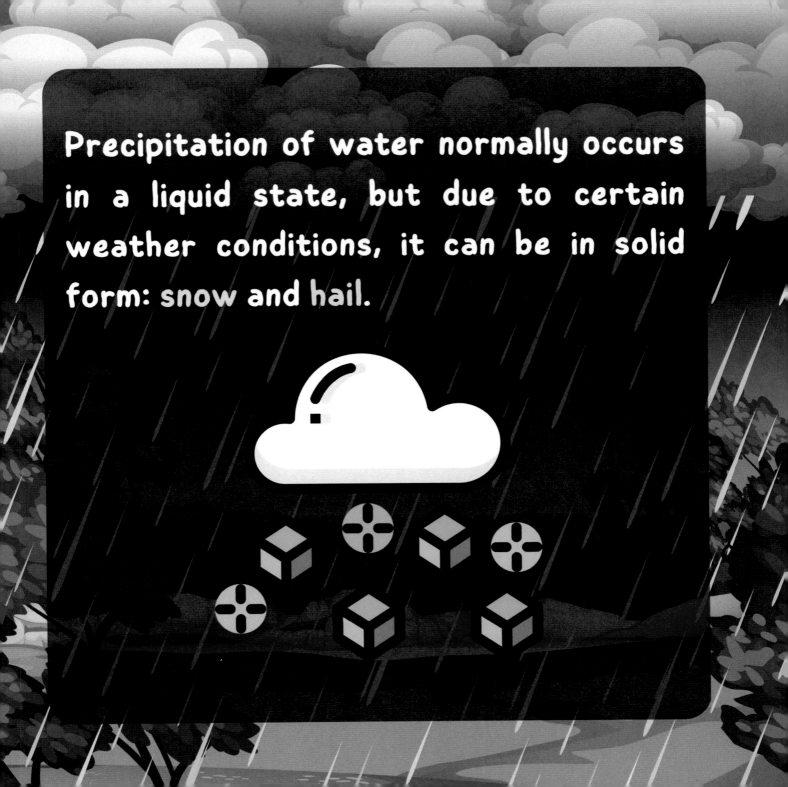

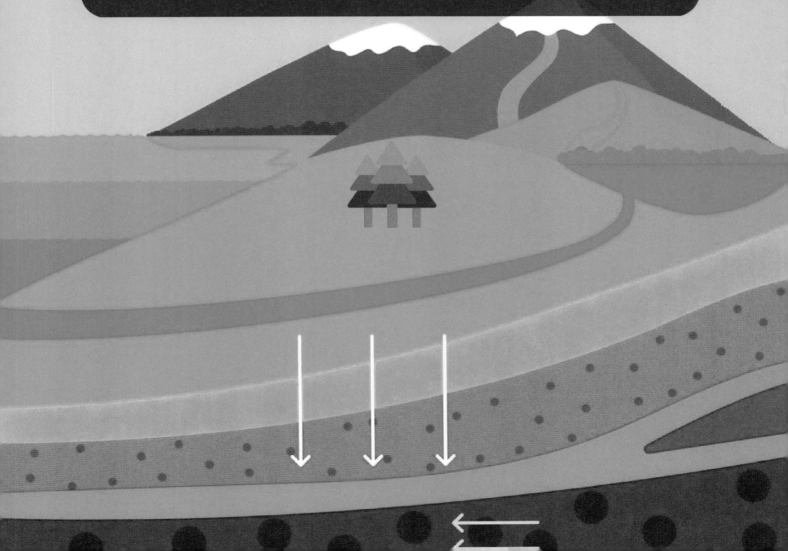

Water from precipitation, rivers, and lakes enters the soil, forming underground water currents.

Part of the water is used by plants and returns to the atmosphere through transpiration.

Another part goes to aquifers, which store large amounts of fresh water that is used by people for consumption and agriculture.

These water reserves help maintain many types of ecosystems, on which populations and species depend.

Another part of the groundwater filters to lower levels and eventually returns to the oceans.

Some of the water coming from precipitation or melting snow moves around the Earth's surface, reaching lakes, rivers, seas, and oceans.

This happens when the land fails to absorb more water or a natural or surface deposit is exceeded.

I want to ask you a favor so that this book reaches more people, and that is that you rate it with a sincere opinion on the platform where you purchased it.

With that small gesture, you will be helping me to carry on with new projects.

I can't wait to start creating my next book for you!

See you soon!

THE WATER CYCLE
For Kids

VOLCANOES
For Kids

HUMAN BODY
Systems

THE MOST >> FAMOUS
Landmarks
IN THE WORLD

DINOSAURS

FASCINATING
UNIVERSE

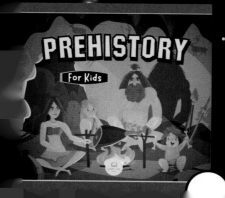

PREHISTORY
For Kids

ANCIENT EGYPT

SCAN ME

I HAVE A GIFT FOR YOU!

This Free eBook is for You!

https://www.bit.ly/samueljohngift

I HOPE YOU LIKE IT!

Samuel John

BOOKS

 contacto@samueljohnbooks.com

 www.facebook.com/bookssamueljohn/

www.amazon.com/author/samueljohnbooks

Made in the USA
Middletown, DE
05 September 2023

38058397R00018